Alvaro Dembuenda

Contribution of the Strategic Program for the Reduction of Urban Poverty

ScienciaScripts

Cover image: www.ingimage.com

This book is a translation from the original published under ISBN 978-620-6-75870-9.

Publisher:
Sciencia Scripts
is a trademark of
Dodo Books Indian Ocean Ltd. and OmniScriptum S.R.L publishing group

120 High Road, East Finchley, London, N2 9ED, United Kingdom
Str. Armeneasca 28/1, office 1, Chisinau MD-2012, Republic of Moldova, Europe

ISBN: 978-620-7-27850-3

Ruben Daniel Ulaia
Octávio Muângelo
Álvaro Dembuenda

Contribution of the Strategic Program for the Reduction of Urban Poverty

Contents

2

Epigraph

"I don't consider myself an expert in either science or
philosophy. I have, however, been trying very hard throughout the
my life, to understand something about the world in
that we live in. Scientific knowledge and rationality
The human beings who produce it are, in my opinion, always fallible
or subject to error. But they are also, I believe, the pride of
humanity. For man is, as far as I know, the only thing
in the universe that tries to understand it. I hope we continue to
do so and that we are also aware of the severe
limitations of all our interventions".

Karl Raimund Popper
(The myth of context)

Dedication

To my firstborn

Kenzo Ruben Ulaia

Thanks

First of all, I would like to thank Almighty God for having enlightened me during these four years of hard work. Thanks go to my parents, Daniel José Ulaia and Fátima Aibo (in memory), siblings, Ulaia Daniel Ulaia, Frank Daniel Ulaia, Dania Daniel Ulaia, Fernando Félix and his family. My special thanks go to my wife Shelsa Virginia Eugénio Balane Ulaia for her companionship, love, passion and friendship on our journey to the fruit of our love Kenzo Ruben Ulaia and Kaseem Eugénio Ruben Ulaia.

To my friends and colleagues on this long journey, for sharing unique and unforgettable moments in our daily lives at the academy and in our community, encouraging each other, with obstacles and without, that the most important thing is to have focus and determination in the goal you want to achieve.

I would also like to thank my teachers, especially my supervisor Professor Octávio Ramos Muangelo, for his teachings, patience and my inspiration in the academic field.

To all those who have helped me grow and become the person I am today.

Summary

Mozambique has shown impressive economic growth and a declining poverty rate over the last 20 years, but 46% of the population still lives in poverty. The unequal availability of basic services, especially in health and education, and obstacles to sustainable employment are at the root of this economic disparity. Social policies focused on combating poverty have therefore been adopted with the aim of reducing this evil. It is within the framework of these efforts that the Strategic Program for the Reduction of Urban Poverty (PERPU) was launched in 2011, covering municipalities and provincial capital cities. This study aims to reflect on the Strategic Program for the Reduction of Urban Poverty (PERPU), with a view to understanding its contribution to improving the living conditions of mayors living in Quelimane. In terms of approach, the study is qualitative. However, it is clear that the situation of poverty in the communities does not seem to have been resolved, given the high levels of deprivation that certain urban families have been experiencing (not having access to basic quality public services and not being able to satisfy them by other means due to lack of financial capacity).

Keywords: *PERPU; Poverty; Citizen; Public Policies.*

CHAPTER I: INTRODUCTION

1.1. Introduction

In Mozambique, the creation of local authorities came about in the context of the decentralization of power, and is necessarily aimed at empowering local leaders and guaranteeing their political and economic autonomy, thereby minimizing the bureaucracies of public administration at central level.

Until the end of the 1990s, Mozambique's urban areas were under the political and administrative authority of the centralized state, both until the end of colonial rule in 1975 and during the period of one-party rule that formally ended with the constitutional revision of 1990.

The new constitutional text established the separation of local government bodies, which now have their own legal personality in relation to the central administrative apparatus.

According to Trindade (2003), cited in Rocha and Zavale (2015):

> Following the constitutional changes, in May 1992 the government approved the Local Bodies Reform Program (PROL), the aim of which was to reformulate the state's local administration system and transform it into local bodies with their own legal personality and endowed with administrative and financial autonomy. As a result, Law 3/94 of 13 September was approved, which established the institutionalization of municipal districts and represented the first regulatory instrument for decentralization (p.111).

In fact, the Territorial Planning Law (Law no.º 19, /2007, of July 18), article 1, defines urban land as all the area within the perimeter of legally established municipalities, towns and villages, seats of administrative posts and localities.

Meanwhile, the "Territorial Planning Policy" (resolution no.º 18, /2007, of 30 May) classifies urban areas taking into account the sustainability of urban centers in terms of urban land use, sanitation and environment, development of transport and communications infrastructures, and housing conditions.

The role that the state plays in our society has undergone numerous transformations over time. In the 18th and 19th centuries, its main objective was public security and external defense in the event of an enemy attack.

However, with the deepening and expansion of democracy, the state's responsibilities have diversified. It is now common to say that the state's role is to promote the well-being of society.

To do this, they need to develop a series of actions and act directly in different areas, such as health, education and the environment.

In order to achieve results in various areas and promote the well-being of society, governments use Public Policies (Sebrae, 2008).

Public policy can be understood, according to Santos (n.d.), as the field of knowledge that seeks, at the same time, to "put the government into action" and/or to analyze this action (independent variable) and, when necessary, to propose changes in the direction or course of these actions and or to understand why or how the actions took a certain course instead of another (dependent variable).

The purpose of this study is to reflect on the Strategic Program for the Reduction of Urban Poverty (PERPU), with the general aim of understanding its contribution to improving the living conditions of mayors living in Quelimane. The work is structured in three chapters:

- ✓ The *first* is reserved for the introduction, which contextualizes the topic, highlights the problem, presents the general and specific objectives, the justification for the problem, the relevance of the study to the scientific and social context, the research questions and finally, the delimitation of the study; the *second* chapter consists of the literature review, which presents the conceptual framework, the theory supporting the theme and the respective theoretical reflection; the *third* chapter presents the methodology used to carry out the study; the *fourth* chapter presents the presentation, analysis and discussion of the results; finally, the *fifth* chapter presents the conclusions of the research and the recommendations for improving the scenario found in the context studied.

1.2. Problematization

Mozambique has demonstrated impressive economic growth and a declining poverty rate over the last 20 years, yet 46% of the population still lives in poverty. The unequal availability of basic services, especially in health and education, and obstacles to sustainable employment are at the root of this economic disparity (Nixon & Walters, 2017).

The 2015/16 survey showed that by 2014 national poverty still stood at 46.1%. This figure represents a drop of 5.6 percentage points since 2008 and a substantial drop of 23.6 points since 1996. However, this comes alongside an increase of over 200% in *per capita* income during the period 1996-2014. This supports the claim that the fruits of economic growth are not "translating" into benefits for many people and that inequality has been increasing (Nixon & Walters, 2017).

In this way, social policies focused on combating poverty have been adopted with the aim of reducing this evil. It is within the framework of these efforts that in the 2011 financial year, the government allocated 140 million Meticais to the Strategic Program for the Reduction of Urban Poverty (PERPU), covering the municipalities and provincial capital cities (Maputo, 2011).

According to Arnaça (2015), the municipalities of Beira and Quelimane have levels that are considered worrying when it comes to repaying the funds granted to borrowers under the Strategic Program for the Reduction of Urban Poverty (PERPU).

From our perspective, the poverty situation around us (in the communities we deal with) doesn't seem to have been resolved, given the deprivations that certain urban families have been experiencing (not having access to quality basic public services and not being able to satisfy them by other means due to lack of financial capacity).

PERPU was designed to complement the government's effort to provide resources to citizens who are unable to go to the bank to take out loans to finance entrepreneurial initiatives and generate income for their survival.

Given the above findings, we ask the following question: *to what extent has the implementation of PERPU in the Quelimane Municipality contributed to improving the lives of citizens and reducing urban poverty?*

1.3. Objectives

1.3.1. General objective

- To analyze the contribution of PERPU in improving the living conditions of citizens in the municipality of Quelimane over the period from 2014 to 2018.

1.3.2. Specific

- Describe how PERPU was implemented in the municipality;
- To assess the performance of the local council in the implementation of PERPU in relation to the levels of poverty found and with regard to the repayment of the funds granted to borrowers;
- Evaluate the urban poverty index in the municipality of Quelimane (2014 to 2018).

1.4. Justification

Considering the speed of demographic growth and the expansion of urban areas, the level of demand for quality public services and access for all is increasing. For this reason, it is important that studies are carried out to analyze and identify mechanisms that guarantee the coverage of public goods and services in Mozambique, in particular to the entire territorial extension of the urban area of the Quelimane Municipal Council, Bearing in mind that this study has political relevance, because it is on the scale of good governance, and social relevance, because it aims to ensure the basic rights of citizens in an equitable manner, equal opportunities for all and, above all, economic relevance, because all these factors condition development and the reduction of urban poverty levels.

1.5. Relevance of the study

Huntington (1994) understands democracy as a regime in which the people are in power, and it is currently seen as the best regime for a society.

Democracy is characterized by equal access to and distribution of wealth, privileging the benefit of the majority and not a small group of people, equal treatment of citizens regardless of party color or political choice, freedom of expression, thought, opinion and information, free, fair and transparent elections.

10

The choice of topic is justified by the fact that it refers to a new reflection on the programs elaborated within the scope of public policies as a way of enriching the study for the field of social sciences, particularly for political science, and in general, for society.

As stated above, access to public services (such as the consumption of public goods) should not be restricted to one social stratum, i.e. they should be available to all citizens, such as public safety, education, health, environmental sanitation, water and electricity distribution networks, among others. It must be said that the distribution and/or availability of services and goods to the public depends first and foremost on formulating and analyzing the directives that make such exercises possible.

In this vein, the study analyzes whether the implementation of the Strategic Program for the Reduction of Urban Poverty in the Quelimane Municipal Council has improved or stimulated the reduction of urban poverty. Hence its relevance.

1.6. Research questions

1. How was PERPU implemented in the Quelimane municipality in terms of selection criteria and lines of action?
2. What is the Urban Poverty Index like in Quelimane Municipality?
3. How has the local council performed in implementing PERPU?

1.7. Delimitation of the Study (Spatial, Temporal, Thematic Framework)

The topic can be delimited by breaking it down into parts. This makes it possible to define the understanding of the terms, which implies explaining the concepts. It can also be done by defining circumstances, time and space. In addition, the researcher can define from which point of view he or she will focus on it (Oliveira, 2011).

As for the spatial approach, the study was carried out in the Quelimane Municipal Council, and as for the temporal approach, it is restricted to the period from 2014 to 2018. In 2014/15, the fourth national poverty assessment was carried out. The 2015/16 survey shows that by 2014, national poverty was still at 46.1% (Nixon & Walters, 2017). (Nixon & Walters, 2017).

11

It can be seen that the results presented in this report show the well-being of the population and a reduction in poverty. On the other hand, the differences between urban and rural areas remain substantial, and in some provinces there is a stagnation or increase in the poverty rate. For these reasons, the aim was to analyze the urban poverty rate in 2014 and 2018 by looking at PERPU's contribution to reducing it.

As for the thematic approach, the study falls within the disciplines of Development, Public Policy and Local Finance, Community Development and Social Services, Public Administration and Political Science.

CHAPTER II: REVIEW OF THE LITERATURE

2.1 Conceptual framework

Program

Program is the written plan of activities for an event. It can also be seen as the list of subjects that are part of a course or that make up the content of a competition. It can also be seen as a written statement explaining the aims and objectives of a political party, a candidate, etc. (Online Dictionary of Portuguese, 2019).

In a general sense, the term *program* refers to something that is planned with the intention of carrying it out later. This word is used in all activities that require a certain amount of prior organization, such as a vacation plan, a study plan, a business strategy, a political proposal, a physical training plan, among others. In general, the program is an enlightening summary of something (Education and Concepts, 2019).

Some are drawn up in a rigorous and systematic way (for example, those that have to do with the business world), while others are a brief summary that highlights a few guidelines. In any case, their development has a dual purpose: to anticipate a situation in advance and to inform others about something. In Portuguese, there are several words that act as synonyms: plano, projeto, esquema, prospecto, esboço (Education and Concepts, 2019).

Strategy

It comes from Greek, more precisely from the Greek words "stratos" and "agem", the first meaning army, the second leading or commanding. The same origin can also be traced to the Greek noun "strategos", which means general. It therefore seems clear that in its origins the word "stratégia" simply meant the action of leading or commanding armies, an action which, as we know, was the responsibility of generals (Martins, 1983).

According to Schnaars (1991, cited in Borges Jr and Luce, 2000), the idea of *strategy* was formally developed by the Greeks, who conceived its concept with a military connotation, in which there was already the idea of an objective to be achieved and action plans to be unleashed in different scenarios according to the enemy's behavior.

Captain Liddel Hart, who proposes the term "grand strategy" for the "art of coordinating and directing all the resources of a nation or a group of nations towards the attainment of the political objective sought by war, and which is defined by politics". (Martins, 1983).

For (Bergue, 2013)strategy can therefore be understood as a set of managerial actions geared towards the desired positioning of an organization in an identified future scenario.

It thus includes the structuring guidelines for management acts, guided by the mission and organizational objectives of a more permanent nature, allowing for the composition of duly integrated sectoral actions.

However, Hasse Filho (2006) emphasizes that strategy can be a perspective, focusing on the fundamental way an organization does things. And finally, strategy can be a trick, that is, a maneuver to deceive or distract a competitor, without the real intention of carrying it out.

Poverty

The conceptualization of *poverty* is extremely complex. It can be made taking into account some "value judgment", in relative or absolute terms. It can be studied only from an economic point of view or by incorporating non-economic aspects into the analysis, and it can be contextualized in a way that is dependent or not on the socio-political structure of society, which will not be explored in this text (Crespo & Gurovitz, 2002).

Asselin (2009, cited in anonymous, n.d.), believes that the concept of poverty has its origins in social ethics, and can be seen as a central part of political philosophy, the field of philosophy that studies the theory of social arrangements. Social ethics is also rooted in moral philosophy. The author argues that thinking about poverty means identifying a situation that is considered unacceptable and unjust in a given society. In this way, the concept of poverty arises from normative considerations of the meaning of justice.

According to the Action Plan for the Reduction of Absolute Poverty (PARPA I) (2001-2005), poverty is "the inability of individuals to ensure for themselves and their dependents a set of minimum basic conditions for their subsistence and well-being, according to the norms of society".

For PARPA II (2006-2009), poverty is "the inability or lack of opportunity of individuals, families and communities to have access to minimum conditions, according to the basic norms of society".

PARP (2011-2014) points out that poverty is a multidimensional phenomenon, and the fight against it is not limited to the elements of absolute poverty, but extends to the broader concept: "The inability or lack of opportunity of individuals, families and communities to have access to minimum conditions, according to the basic norms of society".

For Freitas (2010), poverty represents the absence of choice, a radical lack of resources or a constant deterioration in living conditions. When it comes to basic needs such as housing, health, food or education, those who are deprived of them not only suffer deprivation, but also a serious reduction in their citizenship rights and human rights.

Even though the explanations of this reality come from different analytical matrices, the literature has shown a convergence in the indication of explanatory determinations based on two fundamental axes (Silva, n.d.).

The first points to macroeconomic and structural causes, with emphasis on Gaudier, (1993, cited by Silva, s.d):

a) Global economic crisis, represented by reduced growth, recession, inflation, fluctuating interest rates, loss of dynamism in trade, etc., contributing substantially to the fall in per capita income and the rise in poverty;

b) Internal economic policies with omission in actions to combat poverty, poor administration, inertia and political speculation, combined with external constraints;

c) External debt, which rose sharply during the 1980s, consuming huge resources to service it;

d) Structural adjustment programs imposed by the World Bank and the International Monetary Fund, with high costs for the poor, often without the adoption of programs to minimize budget restrictions and drastic cuts in public spending, especially in social programs, aggravating inequalities, unemployment, housing conditions, health, education, food, reducing social insurance coverage, social services, weakening economic infrastructure, interrupting investments in urban infrastructure, etc;

e) Collapse of socialist economies with extraordinary changes, such as liberalization of the economy, prices and wages, modernization of the wage system, introduction of the idea of competitiveness, privatization measures, undermining the traditional combination of job security, lower wages and more compensatory benefits, without new mechanisms, increasing poverty in these countries to an absurd extent;

f) Industrial restructuring and changes in employment patterns, with the decline of traditional industries; transfer to Third World countries of certain activities with weaker social and ecological standards, cheaper and less organized labor, low taxes; transformation of the remaining productive system, cuts in public services and administration; priority for financial interests over industrial interests, privatization, all contributing to the rise of the "new poverty" - with unemployment, precariousness and fragmentation of work, mainly affecting young people, women and employees of state companies and traditional industries, with enormous growth in the informal sector of the economy.

The second axis of determinants of poverty points to social causes, as Gaudier (1993, cited by Silva, n.d.) points out:

a) Population demographic change with a high population increase in the 1980s, mainly in developing countries, reducing gains in per capita income growth and increasing demands for social services, thus limiting resources for food, health, housing, employment, social services and infrastructure, as well as changes in the distribution of the population with greater urban concentration, migration of certain groups who are forced to accept precarious jobs in sectors without social protection;

b) Economic and social exclusion, highlighted in the literature as a typical mechanism of poverty in industrialized countries, largely contributing to the rise of the 'new poverty', although also pointed out as a phenomenon in developing countries. In addition to the exclusion of certain population groups (children, women, blacks, rural workers, etc.), exclusion by the social protection system is also pointed out as a cause of the increase in poverty;

16

c) Weakening of social solidarity with changes in social patterns and lifestyles, causing the disintegration of the family, considered the main space of solidarity, with an increase in the number of single-parent families, living in precarious situations, as well as the pressure of free market ideology and individualism on mutual protection networks, welfare funds and community systems, traditional supports for the poor.

Seen from this frame of reference, the phenomenon of poverty is discussed in this text by presenting issues of a theoretical and conceptual nature, with emphasis on poverty as a theoretical category, presenting theoretical explanations of a general nature and addressing forms of expression considered here to be typological.

Citizenship

The most distant origin of the idea of citizenship is in what we consider to be Greek democracy, but the real root of the concept is in Rome in the word "civitas", which comes from the republican period, before the Empire, and which means both the condition of citizen and the right to be part of the city as a space and subject that concerned everyone, except slaves and foreigners, since they were not considered citizens (Letria & Letria, 2003) .

Citizenship is a social and historical achievement that must be experienced, especially because it denotes an individual's identity in relation to their fellow human beings. The meaning of the concept of citizenship, as well as its exercise, involves a broad context that needs to be considered for its understanding, clarification and implementation (Pellenz, Bastiani, & Santos, 2015).

According to Pinsky (2003), being a citizen means having the right to life, liberty, property and equality before the law: in short, it means having civil rights. It also means participating in the destiny of society, voting, being voted for, having political rights.

Civil and political rights do not ensure democracy without social rights, those that guarantee the individual's participation in collective wealth: the right to education, to work, to a fair wage, to health, to a peaceful old age. Exercising full citizenship means having civil, political and social rights.

According to Aurélio Buarque (s.d. cited by Rocha, 2000), the definition of a citizen refers to an individual enjoying the civil and political rights of a state, or performing their duties towards it. Social rights are therefore explicitly excluded from this definition. The development of citizenship therefore has little influence on inequality.

Autarchy

The multiple and complex demands of modern life have imposed significant changes on political decision-making mechanisms, which have resulted in the marked development of two legal-political techniques: deconcentration and decentralization.

Deconcentration improves the speed and effectiveness of government action and multiplies the resonance capacity of a single source, the central power, allowing agents dispersed throughout all the administrative districts of the territory to transmit and energize government directives and decide in harmony. (Cosla, n.d.).

Decentralization, in tacit or express recognition of the specificity of local communities, gives them decision-making and administrative capacity in political-administrative areas defined in a legal framework of competences, allowing them to carry out acts that can only be challenged through litigation. (Cosla, n.d.).

Local authorities are autonomous bodies of the Administration, created by law, with legal personality under public law, their own assets and specific state attributions. They are autonomous bodies, but they are not autonomies. Autonomy cannot be confused with autarchy: the former legislates for itself; the latter administers itself, according to the laws issued by the entity that created it (Meireles, n.d.).

According to Meireles (n.d.), an Autarchy is an autonomous dismemberment of the Administration, created by law, with legal personality under public law, internal, its own assets, specific and decentralized state attributions.

In Mozambique, Law n° 2/97 of 28 May (Lei de Bases de Autarquias), in the democratic organization of the state, local power includes the existence of local authorities. Local authorities are public legal entities with their own representative bodies that aim to pursue the interests of their respective populations without prejudice to national interests and state participation. Local authorities carry out their activities within the framework of the unity of the state and are organized with full respect for the unity of political power and the national legal order.

Urban Space

According to Damião (2014), urban space is characterized, first and foremost, by the apprehension that people make of the different land uses that overlap with each other. These uses mark out areas of the city based on their functions: commercial, residential, services, entertainment, etc., and those reserved for the future expansion of the city and capital. "This set of land uses is, in reality, the spatial organization of the city or, simply, urban space, which thus appears as fragmented space."

According to Goncalves, Rothfuss and Morato (2012), in Germany, the characterization of urban spaces is based on principles such as the existence of infrastructure and the provision of minimum public services, even if these principles are not very rigid and with generally determined figures.

For Correa (1995), urban space is the set of different land uses juxtaposed to each other. These uses define areas such as: the city center, where commercial, service and management activities are concentrated; industrial areas and residential areas, distinct in terms of form and social content; leisure areas; and, among others, those set aside for future expansion. This set of land uses is the spatial organization of the city or simply fragmented urban space.

With the intensification of urbanization and its socio-economic and cultural transformations, the spheres of government, with greater responsibility for the local sphere, must provide public policies aimed at organizing urban space to ensure that human activities develop and reproduce in a sustainable manner. (Gonçalves, Rothfuss, & Morato, 2012).

The mobility of the population, be it social, economic or spatial, falls within the sphere of public responsibilities for promoting its development. The absence of these policies, or their implementation without adequate planning, has an impact on the guarantee of fundamental rights and on the reproduction of social structures and relations (Gonçalves, Rothfuss, & Morato, 2012).

Public policies

The concept of Public Policy arose in the United States, rationalizing the actions of public authorities in solving problems. It is nothing more than the planning of the state in the provision of public services to which it is obliged by the constitutional text (Gorczevski & Mayer, 2015).

Mead (1995, cited by Souza, 2002) defines public policy as a field within the study of politics that analyzes government in the light of major public issues.

According to Ham and Hill (1993, cited by Estevão and Ferreira, 2018), the concern with public policies was accentuated in the early 1960s in the United States and originated from two strands of interest:

  I. The difficulties faced by policymakers in the face of the ever-increasing complexity of the problems they faced, leading them to look for ways to build alternatives and proposals for solutions; and

  II. The attention of academic researchers in the social sciences (political science, economics, sociology) who became interested in issues related to public policy in order to apply their knowledge to solving concrete problems in the public sector.

Lynn (1980 cited by Souza, 2002) defines it as a specific set of government actions that will produce specific effects.

Public policies are the totality of actions, goals and plans that governments (national, state or municipal) draw up to achieve the well-being of society and the public interest. It is true that the actions that public leaders (rulers or decision-makers) select (their priorities) are those that they understand to be the demands or expectations of society. In other words, society's well-being is always defined by the government and not by society (Sebrae, 2008).

Peters (1986 cited by Souza, 2002), follows the same vein: public policy is the sum of the activities of governments, which act directly or through delegation, and which influence the lives of citizens.

The definition established by Thomas Dye (1984) is always cited as an acceptable definition of what public policy is, "what the government chooses to do or not to do" (Agum, Riscado, & Menezes, 2015).

2.2. Theoretical Framework

2.2.1 Basic theory

Socio-democratic conception

Social democracy is a model of political and economic organization that agrees, in part, with left-wing ideologies by admitting that the capitalist mode of production has its flaws and shortcomings. But on the other hand, it doesn't believe that capitalism can be eliminated and the best that can be done is to compensate for its shortcomings, advocating the possibility of a humanized capitalism through the conscious action of political forces (such as elections and political reforms) (Medeiros, 2016) .

According to this theory, private control of the means of production forms the basis of the capitalists' ability to exploit labor and impose the dictates of their class interests on the administration of the community's public affairs (Schumpeter, 1961).

Social democrats try to reform capitalism democratically, through state regulation and the implementation of political programs that reduce the social injustices inherent in capitalism (Medeiros, 2016).

The political power of capitalism, therefore, seems to be just a particular form of its economic power. It follows that there can be no democracy as long as this power exists (mere political democracy is simply a deception) and that the elimination of this power will simultaneously end the exploitation of man by man and mark the beginning of the rule of the people (Schumpeter, 1961).

Social democracy is based on the idea that the state should intervene in the economy in order to achieve social justice, but also guided by the criterion of efficiency. An efficient allocation of resources without necessarily transforming the economic system, but by correcting the effects of its operation.

In general, the Welfare State was the political program of the social democrats, "the idea that the state should guarantee equality between individuals came to be seen as a citizen's right" (Sell, 2006, cited in Medeiros, 2016), managing capitalism, adopting an interventionist state model, with an economic program of state control over the market and a social program that ensured basic social rights, such as health, education, social security, protection against unemployment, among others. (Medeiros, 2016).

In the reality under investigation, this theory is justified by the fact that it sees poverty as a phenomenon caused by vices in the distribution of wealth, assuming that in order to overcome the barriers (poverty) it is necessary, in other words, to take from those who have a lot to those who do not. Now, the case of PERPU at municipal level could be one of the alternatives for redistributing wealth since, in our opinion, wage earners or those with a good income are not eligible for the program.

2.2.2.1 Background to the creation of the Strategic Program for the Reduction of Urban Poverty (PERPU)

The emergence of PERPU 2011-2014 is set in a context in which the government's discourse on poverty focused its attention on combating this phenomenon in rural areas, with the introduction in 2006 of the Local Initiative Investment Budget (OIIL), the aim of which is to contribute to poverty reduction by financing individual projects to produce food and generate employment and income (Sande, 2011 cited by Maguenhe 2016).

In the words of Mr. Jeremias Rendição (quoted by Matuassa, 2016), several factors contributed to the emergence of PERPU, among them:

> I-) The increase in urban poverty, especially in peripheral areas; II-) Popular demonstrations in the cities of Maputo and Matola caused by the increase in the cost of living; III-) The lack of employment, transportation and income to meet basic needs; IV-) The rural exodus, which has influenced the high demographic index in the cities, and consequently greater pressure on the labor market; V-) High crime rate and VI-) Complaints from residents about the scope of the District Development Fund, aka 7 million, since this fund only covers rural areas.

In this context, the government felt obliged to create a policy that could solve or minimize the problems mentioned above, adapting the Strategic Program for the Reduction of

Urban Poverty as a solution. Allied to these factors, PERPU emerged through the Government's Five-Year Program (PQG), which includes a set of actions aimed at reducing poverty in general. The 2010-2014 PQG operational document, which in previous mandates was called PARPA, defined the general strategy for reducing both rural and urban poverty.

The Report on the implementation of PERPU during 2015 in Maputo Municipality states that in the 5 municipal districts benefiting from the program, around 457 income generation and job creation projects were approved. This number of projects is an increase of 3% on 2014.

In 2015, 32,673,399.46Mt was available for project financing, which made it possible to finance 457 income-generating projects, in different areas of activity, worth 31,745,563.96Mt and a balance of 9,835.56Mt that was carried over to 2015. This number of projects made it possible to create 1,135 new jobs.

With regard to repayments, the report states that from the start of the program until December 31, 2015, borrowers from the PERPU fund repaid 16,485,124.92Mt, corresponding to 35.6% of the total repayments planned for this period (46,297,463.02Mt).

During 2015, 9.5 million Meticais were reimbursed, which represents an additional 1.04 million Meticais compared to the previous year. During this period, the reimbursement rate was 24.3%, which represents a reduction of 36 pp compared to 2014 and cumulatively the reimbursement rate was 30%, which also represents a reduction of 5.6 pp compared to the previous year.

The same report states that the constraints were the withdrawal of almost all the volunteers who were supposed to work with the District Technical Committees in analyzing the projects, due to a lack of incentives.

In some cases, the Advisory Councils do not know the beneficiaries at the time of collection, while the latter have confirmed the suitability of the beneficiaries when submitting the application to access the PERPU fund.

Lack of knowledge of the suitability of the applicants on the part of the Advisory Board (the main requirement for funding) and misuse of the amounts granted, resulting in non-payment of the installments.

Lack of direct monitoring during the implementation and execution of the projects by the members of the District Advisory Council and the Technical Commission, allegedly due to a lack of circulating resources and materials for monitoring.

Reduction of amounts requested by borrowers for the implementation of their project without prior notice from the DM.

Lack of a beneficiary control system and updated database in the Municipal Districts.

Maguenhe (2016) carried out a study on the Evaluation of the Implementation of the Strategic Program for the Reduction of Urban Poverty (PERPU) in the context of job creation in the KaMubukwana Municipal District (2011-2014). The study essentially aimed to assess the sustainability of the jobs created with the implementation of the program.

In this study, the author carried out bibliographical research and opted for the direct involvement of the main players in the process, favoring previously prepared semi-structured interviews with fifty-five (55) people.

The results of the study revealed that during the implementation of PERPU 2011-2014 in the KaMubukwana Municipal District, 385 projects were funded, spread across different sectors of activity, which contributed to the generation of 912 jobs, with an average of two (2) jobs generated by each project.

According to Maguenhe (2016), the 45 projects visited contributed to the generation of self-employment and some projects generated occasional work in addition to self-employment, coming to the conclusion that they were unsustainable jobs, as there was no legal link between the employer and the employee.

Adolfo (2016) wrote about Public Development Policies: A Look at PERPU as a Women's Empowerment Strategy in the City of Lichinga, the aim of which was to analyze the stages of economic and social development of the women beneficiaries of PERPU.

The problem is to find out to what extent the funds allocated to women through PERPU contribute to the empowerment of women, taking into account their levels of economic and social development.

The study was carried out with a qualitative approach using interview techniques, a bibliographical review in which literature was examined such as managerialism according to Ferlie et al (1999 cited by Adolfo, 2016), the welfare state or the welfare state tending to illustrate the government's concern in creating public gender policies.

The author notes that there is a wide scope for involving women in the process of granting funds to implement projects in the Lichinga municipality, but there is a need to be able to grant these funds to people who are already carrying out their activities and who need support just to get their business back on its feet, as opposed to giving it to someone who has to start, because he understands that if the people who are funded manage to repay the funds, it will be possible for other residents to benefit in the same way and make progress.

As far as the economic and social development of women is concerned, the author states that this is not being felt, as the evidence has shown, for example, that women are managing to support their families through the implementation of their project, but these women still live in precarious conditions.

And finally, the author recommends that women allocate all the value to their projects in a way that is more profitable, so that they can improve in other situations to promote the well-being of their families.

CHAPTER III: METHODOLOGY

This chapter presents the methodology used to prepare the scientific work, subdivided into the type of research, the method used to carry out the research, and finally the techniques used in the data collection process.

Ramos and Naranjo (2013) explain that methodology "is the science that teaches us how to conduct a certain process efficiently and effectively to achieve the desired results and aims to give us the strategy to follow in the process" (p.14).

3.1 Type of research

As for the approach

As for the approach, the research is assumed to be qualitative, according to Marconi and Lakatos (2003), "qualitative methodology is concerned with analyzing and interpreting deeper aspects, describing the complexity of human behavior. It provides a more detailed analysis of research, habits, behavioral trends and other factors" (p.269).

According to Guerra (2014), in the qualitative approach, the scientist aims to deepen their understanding of the phenomena they are studying, the actions of individuals, groups or organizations in their environment or social context, interpreting them according to the perspective of the subjects themselves who participate in the situation, without worrying about numerical representativeness, statistical generalizations and linear cause and effect relationships. We therefore have the following fundamental elements in a research process:

- The interaction between the object of study and the researcher;
- The recording of data or information collected;
- The researcher's interpretation/explanation.

According to Triviños (1987), quoted in Oliveira (2011, p.24), the qualitative approach works with the data to find its meaning, based on the perception of the phenomenon within its context. The use of qualitative description seeks to capture not only the appearance of the phenomenon but also its essence, trying to explain its origin, relationships and changes, and trying to intuit the consequences.

However, according to Nascimento (2016), qualitative research is more appropriate for research in the social sciences. It is based on the interpretation of the phenomena observed and the meaning they carry, or the meaning attributed by the researcher, given the reality in which the phenomena are inserted. It considers the reality and particularity of each research subject.

In terms of objectives

As for the objectives of the research, it is explanatory, because it will explain the causes of the occurrence of the phenomenon to be studied. In this case, it will explain PERPU's contribution to improving citizens' living conditions and reducing urban poverty in the Quelimane municipality over the period from 2014 to 2018.

According to Gil (1999, cited by Oliveira, 2011), the basic aim of explanatory research is to identify the factors that determine or contribute to the occurrence of a phenomenon. It is the type of research that deepens the knowledge of reality, as it tries to explain the reason and the cause and effect relationships of phenomena.

According to Lakatos & Marconi (2001, cited by Oliveira, 2011), this type of research aims to establish cause-and-effect relationships through the direct manipulation of variables related to the object of study, seeking to identify the causes of the phenomenon.

As for methodological procedures

In terms of procedures, it is a *case study*. The term case study was coined by France's le Play (1855), who first used it to study working families in France. The method is based on the principle that one (any) case, studied in depth, can be considered representative of many other cases, or even of all the same or similar cases. The method consists of studying individuals, professions, conditions, institutions, social groups or communities, with the aim of obtaining generalizations (Lundin, 2016).

According to Gil (2008, p. 58), a case study is characterized by the in-depth and exhaustive study of one or a few objects, in order to allow a broad and detailed knowledge of them, a task that is practically impossible with the other types of design considered.

Freitas and Jabbour (2011), conclude that the case study is an empirical investigation that investigates a contemporary phenomenon within its real-life context" appropriate when "the circumstances are complex and can change, when the conditions that concern them have not been encountered before, when the situations are highly politicized and where there are many stakeholders.

However, according to Yin (2005) cited in Lima, Antunes, Neto and Peleias (2012), "the use of a case study is appropriate when the aim is to investigate the how and why of a set of contemporary events. The author states that the case study is an empirical investigation that allows the study of a contemporary phenomenon within its real-life context, especially when the boundaries between the phenomenon and the context are not clearly defined" (p.132).

However, it is along these lines that we have chosen to study a public policy. In a way, in order to analyze the impact of implementing a public policy, it is necessary to meet the actors for whom the respective public policy was drawn up, in this case society.

3.2 Universe and sample

In general, social surveys cover such a large universe of elements that it is impossible to consider them in their entirety. For this reason, in social research it is very common to work with a sample, i.e. a small part of the elements that make up the universe. This is particularly the case in surveys or experiments (Gil, 2008).

According to Marconi and Lakatos (2003), "universe or population is the set of animate or inanimate beings that have at least one characteristic in common" (p.223).

According to Gil (2008), a universe or population is a defined set of elements that have certain characteristics. Population is commonly referred to as the total number of inhabitants of a given place. For this research, the target population was considered to be the mayors of the city of Quelimane, a total of 359,194 thousand.

There are two major divisions in the sampling process: non-probabilistic and probabilistic (Marconi & Lakatos, 2003).

According to Gil (2008), "a sample is a subset of the universe or population through which the characteristics of that universe or population are established or estimated. And in this research project it will be based on non-probabilistic sampling by accessibility or convenience" (p.90).

The author goes on to say that non-probability sampling allows the researcher to select the elements to which they have access, assuming that these can, in some way, represent the universe. This type of sampling is used in exploratory or qualitative studies, where a high level of precision is not required.

However, once the population had been defined, it was deemed important to interview 1 manager of the fund department for poverty reduction in the municipality of Quelimane, 5 PERPU borrowers and 35 individuals from different families distributed in equal numbers in the 5 administrative posts.

3.3 Data Collection Techniques and Instruments

In the data collection process, a combination of three instruments will be used: bibliographical research, documentary data collection, interviews and observation.

Bibliographical research

According to Marconi and Lakatos (2009), "bibliographical research can either be an independent piece of work or be the initial step in another piece of research. It has already been said here that all scientific work presupposes preliminary bibliographical research" (p.115).

According to Gil (1999), bibliographical research is carried out on the basis of material that has already been prepared, consisting mainly of books and scientific articles. The main advantage of bibliographical research lies in the fact that it allows the researcher to cover a much wider range of phenomena than could be researched directly. Its purpose is to put the researcher in touch with what has already been produced and recorded about the research topic.

Documentary research

However, documentary research is a way of passing on the testimony of those who have researched in the same field before, into our hands. Studying what has been produced in the same area is therefore not an affirmation of academic erudition or some intellectual pendantism, but an act of information management, which is indispensable for anyone who wants to add some value to existing scientific production without running the risk of studying what has already been studied, taking what others have already discovered as original. (Carmo & Ferreira, 2008).

According to Gil (2008) "documentary research is very similar to bibliographical research. The essential difference between the two lies in the nature of the sources: while bibliographical research makes fundamental use of the contributions of various authors, documentary research makes use of materials that have not yet received an analytical treatment and can be reworked according to the objects of the research" (p.51).

In the view of Castilho, Borges and Tanús (2014), documentary research is research based on the collection of data from written or unwritten documents, through primary sources, carried out in libraries, research institutes and centers, museums, private collections (churches, schools, banks, health centers, registry offices, hospitals) and public collections (documents from official bodies such as official letters, laws, deeds) and others such as statistical sources, legal sources, etc.

Interview

The interview, which is one of the main data collection techniques in the social sciences, is an important tool for complementing information from reading the literature or observing reality, as well as for gathering information about individuals' experiences or systems of values and representations.

The interaction with a multiplicity of actors, inserted in different contexts and realities and with different types of capital, allows the researcher to capture different ideas, opinions, discourses and positions on the object of research (Feijó, 2017).

For Lundin (2016), the interview is a direct contact between the researcher and the researched in order to obtain relevant information (primary sources) from the latter through a more or less structured conversation. (Lundin, 2016).

For Carmo and Ferreira (2008), the overall aim of any interview is to start by reducing our secret area by applying a fundamental rule of human relations, the rule of reciprocity:

> Direct interaction is a key issue in the interview technique. The usual situation at the start of an interview is the presence of two interlocutors (two windows) whose interaction has very small free areas, relatively large blind areas and equally large secret areas. In other words, when an interview begins, the researcher has usually shared little information with the interviewee (small free area), knows little about them (large blind area of the interviewer and secret area of the interviewee) and the interviewee is in the same situation (extensive blind area of their own and secret area of the interviewer).

Ramos & Naranjo (2013) "the interview is a technique for gathering information through a professional conversation which also provides information about what is being investigated. It is important from an educational point of view. The results to be obtained in the mission depend to a large extent on the level of communication between the researcher and the participants in the interview" (p.141).

According to Marconi and Lakatos (2010) cited in Guerra (2014), with the use of interviews, you can:

- Investigate what happened;
- Find out what people think about the facts;
- Know the person's feelings about the fact or its meaning for them;
- Finding out what people's behavior was, is or would be, whether past, present or planned (future);
- Discovering factors that influence people's thoughts, feelings or actions.

Observation

The other technique used was simple observation. According to Marconi and Lakatos (2009), "observation is a data collection technique for obtaining information using the senses to obtain certain aspects of reality. It consists not only of seeing and hearing, but also of examining facts or phenomena that one wishes to study. It is a basic element of scientific investigation, used in field research and constitutes the fundamental technique of anthropology" (p.275).

According to Gil (2014), "simple observation is when the researcher, while remaining uninvolved in the community, group or situation they intend to study, spontaneously observes the facts that occur there. In this procedure, the researcher is much more of a spectator than an actor. That's why it can be called observation - reportage, since it presents a certain similarity to the techniques employed by journalists" (p.101).

3.4 Data Analysis and Validation Techniques and Instruments

For the analysis and validation of data in this research on the impact of PERPU, the triangulation method will be used.

Denzin and Lincoln (2006) cited in Bruchez and Antonio (2015), Triangulation is a safe way to validate research. It is the alternative to employing multiple methodological practices, perspectives and observers in the same research, which guarantees rigor, richness and complexity to the study.

The use of multiple sources of evidence in case study research allows the researcher to address a wider range of historical and behavioral aspects, developing converging lines of inquiry. In this way, any conclusion from the case study is more convincing, and needs to be grounded in several different sources of information (Bruchez & Antônio, 2015).

According to Maxwell (1996) cited in Azevedo and Abdalla (2013) triangulation "reduces the risk that the conclusions of a study reflect biases or limitations typical of a single method" and therefore leads to "more credible conclusions".

According to Marcondes and Brisola (2014), when it comes to data collection, triangulation allows the researcher to use three or more techniques in order to broaden the information universe around their research object, using, for example, focus groups, interviews, questionnaires, among others.

3.5 Limitations of the study

Carrying out a case study is not an easy task, it requires time and dedication on the part of the researcher and often "the work is subject to criticism due to methodological limitations in the choice of case(s), data analysis and the generation of conclusions supported by the evidence" (Freitas and Jabbour, 2011).

Limitations in the process of this research may also include access to material information, the location of PERPU beneficiaries and financial conditions for travel, i.e. transportation.

According to Yin (2005) cited in Freitas and Jabbour (2011), despite its limitations, the case study is the most suitable method for gaining in-depth knowledge of all the nuances of a given organizational phenomenon. In this sense, even when conducting a single case, some generalizations can be attempted when the context involves decisive, rare, typical, revealing and longitudinal cases.

3.6. Ethical aspects

According to Cortina and Martinez (2005), the word ethics comes from the Greek ethos, originally meaning "dwelling", "place in which one lives" and later meaning "character", "way of being" that one acquires during life.

For Neme and Santos (2012), ethics discusses the values that translate into happier, more fulfilled human existences, with greater well-being and quality of life. It also seeks values that signify dignity, freedom, autonomy and citizenship.

Ethics in research must permeate all the researcher's work. With the advent of the internet, there has been a proliferation of plagiarism and copying of texts without citing the source of the search, thus disrespecting the authors. (Del-Masso, Cotta, & Santos, n.d.).

Lundin (2016), in his approach to ethics in scientific research with a focus on the social and political sciences, brings to mind five important aspects in the research process:

- **Cost and Benefit in the Process/Result of Research Work:** the question to be asked about what is gained and what is lost thus has a high degree of pertinence, whether for the researcher, for the researched/interviewed/observed, for individuals, for the social groups in which they belong, or for the clients who commission research.

- **Consented information:** as an ethical principle, the student/researcher must do everything possible to ensure that the information provided by the subject/target group is consented to, which implies respect for cultural and legal issues that often cannot be universally codified.

- **Privacy of the Subject as the Object of Research:** the right to privacy is a human right. This is an old and recurring problem for researchers today, mainly because, with the use of information, the data collected in a research project can sometimes be used for purposes other than those originally outlined by the researcher and can even be used by researchers other than those who originally set up the project.

- **Anonymity and confidentiality:** in the classic case of anonymity, the researcher separates the information from the identity of the subject providing the information. They work with codes that can be assigned from the outset, using an existing statistic where even the researcher is unaware of the subject's identity and knows only the relevance of the information to their work. Confidentiality is usually promised and guaranteed by researchers to their interviewees, when this is necessary and relevant.

This research will strive to carefully comply with the ethical principles observed above, so that at the end of it, its validity will be credible and referential in the field of public policy studies.

CHAPTER IV: PRESENTATION, ANALYSIS AND DISCUSSION OF RESULTS

This chapter is essentially reserved for data analysis and interpretation. It takes into account the analysis variables for calculating the multidimensional poverty index currently adopted by the United Nations Development Program (UNDP), developed in partnership with the Oxford Poverty & Human Development Initiative (OPHI). (Vaz, 2014).

To achieve **specific objective 1,** the **main variables** were: criteria for selecting beneficiaries, frequency of funding, frequency of monitoring and evaluation.

For **specific objective 2, the main variables**: household size (number of men and women), household income levels, social situation or characteristics of the family (levels of formal education, malnutrition in the family), existence of vulnerable age groups in the family (children, the elderly and women).

Standard of living (Family without electricity, family without access to clean drinking water, family without access to adequate sanitation, house with dirt floor, family uses "dirty" fuel for cooking (dung, firewood or charcoal), family has no car and owns at most one of the following: bicycle, motorcycle, radio, refrigerator, telephone or television.

For **specific objective 3,** the **main variables for analysis** are: poverty levels before and after PERPU, and the strategies and procedures adopted for reimbursing the funds.

4.1. Presentation of results

At this point in the study, the data collected is presented. According to Oliveira (2011), in this context, the data collected by the empirical research should be presented, based on the data collection process. The description of the data can be supported by statistical resources, tables and graphs, drawn up during the tabulation of the data, as well as tables that summarize the description of the results.

If a questionnaire is used, the frequency, percentages, averages and standard deviations of the answers can be described, or graphs can be used to describe the answers. In the case of interviews, describe the categories of answers that appeared (Oliveira, 2011).

4.1.1 Description of the Quelimane Municipal Authority

Quelimane Municipal Council is the capital of Zambezia province, located on the northern bank of the Bons Sinais River, about 18 km from the coast, and at an altitude of no more than 100 meters above sea level. The city is famous for its mild climate and the quality of its soil. It is located in a coastal area and borders the district of Nicoadala to the north and west, the district of Inhassunge to the south and the Indian Ocean to the east (MAE, 2002 cited by Virgílio 2013).

Quelimane means Mount in Swahili, as the natives said they came from Mount Limane when the Portuguese arrived. Thus, it is possible that the African interpreters who accompanied Vasco da Gama, knowing the meaning of the prefix Qui in the Bantu language, when they heard the Chuabos calling themselves Limane, started calling them Qui-limane, which means those who say, speak Limane (idem).

Another version says that when the Portuguese first landed in Porto, which later became Quelimane, the village chief, of Muslim descent, acted as an interpreter between the Portuguese and the locals. In Swahili kaliman means interpreter. There are also those who derive the term from culima, which means to cultivate in various Bantu languages (idem).

In legal terms, the Council was created on May 9, 1761, elevated to the category of City on August 21, 1940 (Ministerial Diploma no. 1/42). In 1763 the village was elevated to the category of Town, with the right to a Town Council, although it functioned as a Municipal Commission between 1897-1942 (idem).

In 1994 the town of Quelimane was elevated to the category of Municipal District, in harmony with Law no. 2/97 by which it was elevated to the category of Municipality.

4.1.2 Process of implementing PERPU in the Quelimane Municipality

4.1.2.1 Data from the Interview with the Accounts Manager of the Urban Poverty Reduction Fund Department in the Municipality of Quelimane

For the presentation of the interview data, in this subchapter the respondents have been coded in order to safeguard the ethics of the research, especially the principle of not identifying the respondents by name, for example G (accounts manager of the Department of the Urban Poverty Reduction Fund in the Municipality).

Asked **what criteria were adopted for selecting PERPU beneficiaries**, we received the following response:

G: "In order to implement PERPU, the technical team suggests that each borrower design their own project, submit it to the municipal council for consideration; once the project has been approved, they will be given the form to fill in and attach the necessary documentation for this purpose and submit it to the advisory council of their neighborhood. (...) it is these advisory councils that define with the community what the relevant needs are in that area, once again they are instructed what steps to follow in order to be able to adhere to these funds to be implemented in the territory of the Municipal District and which must favor the sustainable use of local resources, human, material and natural resources".

Asked **what amount has been granted to the Quelimane Municipal Council for the implementation of PERPU?** We obtained the following answer:

G: "The Urban Poverty Reduction Program has been implemented since 2011. To this end, the government has disbursed an annual amount of 10,350,790.00 meticais to finance small, medium and large income projects."

For the question regarding the number of projects created and approved in the period 2014 to 2018, we obtained the data that we structured below based on the table below.

Table 1: How many projects and jobs were approved and created between 2014 and 2018?

Year	Jobs	Projects created	Approved Projects
2014	405	Poultry farming, Commerce, Carpentry, Fishing, Salon.	304

201 5	440	Poultry, Commerce, Carpentry, Livestock.	390
201 6	485	Poultry farming, Commerce, Carpentry, Salon/Beauty salon.	452
201 7	470	Poultry farming, Commerce, Carpentry, Metalwork	461
201 8	463	Poultry farming, Commerce, Affectaria, Mechanics. Hairdresser	463

Source: Author

Are these jobs and projects sustainable (do they still exist today)? We obtained the following from this question:

G: "From 2014 to 2018 there are some sustainable jobs and projects for the Quelimane municipality."

To the question **Has the level of poverty decreased?** We obtained the following answer:

G: The Quelimane Municipality has reduced urban poverty.

How? (What are the factors that indicate an improvement in the lives of citizens in the Municipality of Quelimane?) This question was answered as follows:

G: "Increased employment opportunities and levels of employability of the workforce, improved the lives of the residents of Quelimane, increased employment opportunities, improved the business environment, improved the self-employment protection system, including the informal sector, promotion of small and medium-sized enterprises, basic social, increasing improvement of the business environment."

4.1.2.2 Successes in implementing PERPU

The implementation of the projects in the municipality of Quelimane has had significant impacts, with a particular focus on the communities. There has been a reduction in the distance that the population traveled to buy basic necessities, and the food production projects have boosted the sustainable increase in production and productivity levels, including: an increase in family income, an increase in purchasing power, an improvement in life and well-being, the creation of new jobs and self-employment, and the rehabilitation and construction of their homes using conventional materials.

What mechanisms were used for the repayment of the Fund by borrowers?

The beneficiaries of the program's resources are called upon within the agreed deadlines to repay the debt, doing so by deposit or bank transfer to an account previously indicated by the Municipal Authorities.

If the repayment is made by deposit or bank transfer, the beneficiary submits the document proving this operation and, in return, receives a document confirming receipt of the amount in question for all forms of repayment.

Once the loan has been repaid in full, the municipal authorities issue the beneficiary with a discharge certificate.

The debt repayment period may be renegotiated by the beneficiary with the municipal authorities when external factors beyond the beneficiary's control occur, such as natural disasters, and confirmed by the local authorities.

In the event of non-compliance with the stipulated deadlines, the legal mechanism must be activated in accordance with the provisions of the contract.

Beneficiaries who fully comply with the loan agreement are barred from receiving another loan and their name must be communicated to other similar funds operating in the country.

4.1.2.3 Data from the interview with PERPU borrowers in the Municipality of Quelimane

Table 2: Economic Activity

Question	Respondent	Answer
	M1	Trade (sale of used clothes, bale)
	M2	Trade (bar and basic necessities)

	M3	Trade (basic necessities)
What do you do?	M4	Trade (basic necessities and a small hardware store)
	M5	Trade (basic necessities and bar)

Source: Author

Table 1Knowledge about the existence of PERPU

Question	Respondent	Answer
	M1	the municipality's employees began to report;
	M2	I realized from the people that they were after this money. Then I went to the neighborhood secretary to find out how to get the money;
	M3	it was on the basis of the neighborhood secretary;
How did you hear about the Strategic Program for the Reduction of Urban Poverty (PERPU)?	M4	colleagues in the business area who were going to take this money and I also went to the secretary of the neighborhood to find out what was needed and submitted my project.
	M5	it was through friends, we applied, a group was organized to raise that amount of 100,000.00 meticais and then we started to distribute it.

Source: Author

Table 2Amount granted for project implementation

Question	Respondent	Answer
	M1	28,000.00 meticais
	M2	30,000.00 meticais

How much have you been given to implement your project?	M3	25,000.00 meticais
	M4	25,000.00 meticais
	M5	20,000.00 meticais

Source: Author

Table 3Level of Satisfaction with the amounts granted

Question	Respondent	Answer
Was the amount enough to start your project?	M1	was not enough, because of the high standard of living of the agira, the increase in things.
	M2	It was enough, but it's not what I wanted, but as it's in the owner's pocket and they say they can only give that, I can only receive it.
	M3	It wasn't enough, I asked for a certain amount and they reduced it, it wasn't good.
	M4	It wasn't enough, it was too small for the type of business I wanted.
	M5	It was enough for me at the time the division was made, I don't know for the others.

Source: Author

Table 4Did the PERPU grant solve the family's housing, water, clothing, food, education and health problems?

Question	Respondent	Answer

	M1	It's worth getting, but it hasn't solved all my problems, it's normalized enough to get by.
	M2	It's worth it, it's solved a few problems
Is it worth it to be a creditor of this fund (it has solved the family's housing, water, clothing, food, education and health problems)?	M3	Yes, it's worth it, my house hasn't improved, but I've gotten some material to be able to rehabilitate it, now I can pay for water, energy too, to buy food and school to buy uniforms, notebooks.
	M4	It's worth it, the money is there to bet on, but solving the problems isn't easy, but we're making progress little by little, the needs are many.
	M5	It's worth it for those of us who don't have a job, and it's helped my daughters' studies, to pay for water, energy and other things we need to survive, but it's a pain in the ass because you have to pay it back every month even though you haven't produced anything.

Source: Author

Table 5Problems Faced in Project Implementation

Question	Respondent	Answer
	M1	Rising prices on the market, very low turnover, how to return the amount, so far I've only managed to return 5,000.00 meticais.
	M2	After receiving the money, I went shopping and a few days later I was

		robbed. I went to the police station to report it, but to this day nothing has happened.
What problems did you face when implementing your project?	M3	Lack of sufficient funds to leverage the business, he had already started with the business, but the fund was to boost his business further.
	M4	No problems, I already had skills and I have many in the business area, it's an area I've been working in for a long time and you can adapt to reality little by little.
	M5	With the reinforcements on either side, it's possible to walk a little at a time.

Source: Author

Table 6 Life before and after joining PERPU

Question	Respondent	Answer
	M1	I've always been a used-clothing salesman and life is still the same, I haven't progressed.
	M2	Before it was normal, but since I took the money with the products going up on the market, life is getting complicated, we didn't count when we took the money that the prices were going to go up from here to here.
What was your life like before and after joining this program?	M3	My life before and after has always been business, from sixth grade until now.

	M4	This money came just to help my business, but to say that it changed nothing much. Life doesn't change from here to here.
	M5	Life goes on just like that, pushing on, trying other things in order to survive.

Source: Author

Table 7Point of View on the Criteria for the Selection and Approval of Projects

Question	Respondent	Answer
	M1	were good.
	M2	was good.
	M3	were not complicated, it just depends on one's luck.
What is your point of view on the criteria for selecting and approving projects to access the fund?	M4	are normal.
	M5	normal

Source: Author

4.1.4 Data Exhibition for Families living in the Municipality of Quelimane

In carrying out the study, it was considered pertinent to assess the level of poverty in the communities and to find out if they had any knowledge of the existence of the Strategic Program for the Reduction of Urban Poverty, which was carried out in the five administrative posts of Quelimane, designated as administrative posts 1, 2, 3, 4 and 5, in which 7 surveys were distributed.

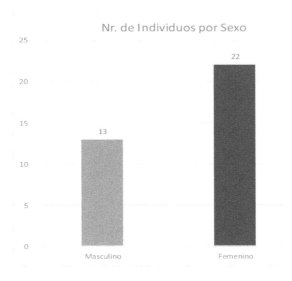

Graph 1 Number of Individuals by Sex

In the survey, 35 people were interviewed, 13 men and 22 women. Of these, 6 belonged to the 15 to 24 age group, 24 to the 25 to 54 age group, 4 to the 55 to 64 age group and 1 to the 65 and over age group, as shown in the graph below.

Graph 2 Number of Individuals by Age Group

45

With regard to specialized activity within the community, of the 35 individuals surveyed, 23% are farmers, 17% are students, 17% work in the home, 26% are unemployed, 8% are private sector workers and 9% are public sector workers.

Graph 3 Number of individuals by profession

With regard to education, 20% of respondents have already completed elementary school, 37% have not yet completed elementary school, 29% have completed secondary school, and 14% of respondents have not yet completed secondary school.

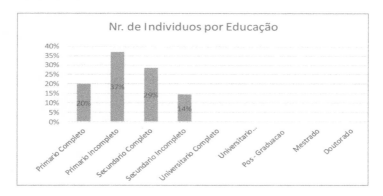

Graph 4: Schooling

46

With regard to the standard of living of those interviewed, 14% of families do not have access to electricity in their homes, 49% of families do not have access to piped drinking water, 100% of them do not have access to adequate sanitation, 23% of the homes surveyed do not have a dirt floor, 37% use firewood for cooking, 100% of those interviewed use charcoal for cooking, 66% have access to a radio, 100% of families have access to a basic telephone for communication, 14% do not have a fridge and finally 17% have a television.

Graph 5 Standard of Living

Asked if they had ever heard of PERPU, 6% of respondents said they had heard of it and 94% had never even heard of the Strategic Program for the Reduction of Urban Poverty.

Graph 6: Consultation on the PERPU

4.2. Analysis and Discussion of Results

At this stage, the data collected by the research is analyzed and discussed. Oliveira (2011) recommends that at this stage the researcher should draw up an analysis based on the results achieved and on the literature review. Attention should be drawn to new and interesting aspects that have emerged. Discussing results means analyzing them and comparing them with previous research.

To materialize PERPU, the government has disbursed 10,350,790.00 meticais annually to finance small, medium and large income projects in the municipality of Quelimane. With regard to job creation, respondent **G** said that from 2014 to 2018 a total of 2,070 jobs were created, most of which were in carpentry, fishing, hairdressing, poultry farming, carpentry, fishing, livestock farming, locksmithing, carpentry, mechanics, with a greater focus on the sale of basic necessities.

With regard to the perception of the activity they carry out, the borrowers referred to as M1, M2, M3, M4 and M5 use commerce as an activity to create income for their sustainability, with M1 selling used clothes, commonly known as fardo, M2 sells alcoholic and non-alcoholic beverages, M3 sells basic necessities, M4 also sells basic necessities and has a small hardware shop, and finally M5 sells basic necessities and alcoholic and non-alcoholic beverages (Table.1).

According to our respondent (G), the implementation of these projects has had a significant impact, with a particular focus on the communities. There has been a reduction in the distance people travel to buy basic necessities, and the food production projects have boosted the sustainable increase in production and productivity levels.

With regard to Table 2, when it comes to the borrowers' knowledge of the existence of PERPU, M1 found out about the existence of the fund through officials from the municipal council who passed on the information. M2 found out about it through members of his community who were attracted to join the fund, and another source of information was the neighborhood secretary who instructed him on how to obtain the funding, as did M3. M4 heard about it from his colleagues in the business and also from the neighborhood secretary, like M2 and M3, and finally M5 heard about it from friends.

48

However, it can be seen that the secretaries of the neighborhoods played a leading role in the dissemination and instruction for the granting of the funds made available by PERPU, with an emphasis on interpersonal communication.

With regard to the amounts granted for the implementation of the projects, it can be seen from table 3 that they vary between twenty thousand meticais (20,000.00) and thirty thousand meticais (30,000.00). When asked if this amount was enough, the borrowers, M1, M3 and M4, were unanimous in declaring that these amounts are not enough. One of the reasons for this is the increase in the standard of living, which means that the prices seen during the period when the projects were being drawn up end up inflating their implementation. The other issue is that PERPU managers have reduced the figures without taking into account the needs already set out in the project.

And the report on the implementation of PERPU in 2015 in the Municipality of Maputo emphasizes this issue of the reduction of amounts requested by borrowers for the implementation of their projects without prior notice from the Municipal District, which ends up being an obstacle to their materialization and success.

Borrowers M2 and M5 were unanimous in saying that it was enough, but with their own assumptions, in which the former said it wasn't the amount he had sent and had to adjust to the amount financed, and the latter said it was enough at the time he received the financing and not afterwards.

However, it is true to say that the amounts granted by PERPU were not and are not enough to start projects aimed at creating basic income to reduce poverty rates. Poverty in this context is defined and analyzed from the perspective of the PARP (2011-2014) as "the inability or lack of opportunity of individuals, families and communities to have access to minimum conditions, according to the basic norms of society".

When asked if it was worth being a creditor of the fund and if it had solved any issues such as housing, water, clothing, food, education and family health problems, all the borrowers (M1, M2, M3, M4, M5) were unanimous in saying that it was worth betting on the fund, But their basic problems have not been solved in their entirety. For example, interviewee M1 said that the money was only enough to survive on, and M3, although he hasn't managed to get enough money to build an improved house, has managed to buy some material to renovate his current home.

Adolfo (2016, *op. cit.*) states that the economic and social development of women with the implementation of PERPU is not felt in his study group, referring to the fact that these women do manage to support their families, but on the other hand they live in precarious conditions.

Paradoxically to the idea mentioned above, respondent **G**'s statements ensure that the implementation of PERPU has increased job opportunities and the employability levels of the workforce, there is an improvement in the lives of the residents of Quelimane, increased job opportunities, improved the business environment, improved the self-employment protection system, including the informal sector, the promotion of small and medium-sized enterprises, basic social, the increasing improvement of the business environment.

Interviewees M4 and M5 say that it's not easy to solve all the problems, but that life progresses gradually and that the fund helps to some extent to meet some basic needs such as education, the purchase of energy and medicines, but the biggest stumbling block is the issue of repayment.

Maguenhe's (2016) evaluation of the implementation of PERPU in the context of job creation in the KaMubukwana Municipal District states that of the 45 projects visited, they contributed to the creation of self-employment and some projects, in addition to self-employment, created occasional work, coming to the conclusion that they were unsustainable jobs in that there was no legal link between the employer and the employee.

With this in mind, the borrowers were asked about the main problems they faced when implementing their projects. Interviewee M1 pointed out that the problem was the increase in market prices, the lack of clients, the issue of disbursement not being proportional to monthly earnings, often having to hand over the same, which ended up conditioning the business.

Interviewee M2 said that one of his constraints was the theft he suffered after buying the material for the execution and implementation. Borrower M3's problem was the lack of sufficient funds to boost his business, as he had already been doing business and the funds were to boost his business further. M4 didn't have any problems because he was already skilled in the business and knew how to adapt to the economic fluctuations in Mozambique. Finally, interviewee M5 had to deal with relapses due to lack of clients and often resorted to other funds to avoid going bankrupt.

Adolfo (2016), calls for these funds to be granted to people who are already developing their activities and who need support just to get their business back on its feet, as opposed to giving it to someone who will have to start, because he understands that if the people who are funded manage to repay the funds, other residents will be able to benefit in the same way and progress.

When asked what life was like before and after joining PERPU, M1, M2, M3, M4 and M5 were unanimous in saying that their lives have always been based on business and that the financial amounts granted by PERPU were simply to assist and help galvanize their businesses.

In our view, they would not be eligible, given the standards of living presented above, because PERPU is intended to support vulnerable but economically active people who do not have access to bank credit or other types of credit granted by formal financial institutions. This population group includes young people, women - heads of households, including widows and disabled people who are able to work.

In recent years, there has been a growing consensus that poverty is a multidimensional phenomenon, involving other dimensions besides consumption, such as access to and quality of health and education, housing, ownership of durable goods, freedom, etc. (UNDP, 2010).

The consumption and multidimensional approaches provide information on different characteristics of poverty, and therefore their estimates can be seen as complementary. It is possible, for example, that a given family or individual faces deprivation in relation to consumption, but not in relation to other dimensions such as health, education or housing, and vice versa (IOF, 2016).

With regard to the standard of living of the families interviewed, 14% are families that do not have access to electricity in their homes; 49% correspond to families without access to piped drinking water, 100% of them do not have access to adequate sanitation, 23% of the homes of the individuals surveyed have a dirt floor, 37% use firewood for cooking, 100% of those interviewed use charcoal for cooking, 66% of families have access to a radio, 100% of families have access to a basic telephone for communication, 14% do not have a fridge and finally 17% have a television, which means that poverty has not yet decreased, i.e. that most of the individuals surveyed live in multidimensionally poor families.

It is clear that the situation of poverty in the communities does not seem to have been resolved, given the deprivations that certain urban families have been experiencing (not having access to quality basic public services and not being able to satisfy them by other means due to lack of financial capacity).

When these families were asked if they had ever heard of PERPU, most of them had never heard of the existence of a program whose aim is to provide them with the financial means to start an activity that can guarantee them a minimum income to meet their basic needs.

Finally, when asked what their point of view was regarding the selection and approval criteria for the projects, the aim of which is to contribute to poverty reduction by financing individual food production and job and income generation projects, borrowers M1, M2 were unanimous in saying that they were good, M3 that they were not complicated and that the approval process had to do with the divine issue of each applicant, M4 and M5 agreed that they were normal.

The UNDP report (2010, *op. cit.*), among other things, discusses the causes (or factors) of poverty in the world: Natural factors - climate, soil desertification; demographic (biological) factors, i.e. that rapid population growth is the biggest obstacle to economic progress and the well-being of citizens; social factors, i.e. the low level of education and inclusion of the population; political factors, i.e. the absence of good governance and democratic institutions, widespread corruption, etc.; economic factors, i.e. low levels of savings, lack of investment, maladjusted tax system, economic disruption.

However, from the data analyzed here, we see that the factors described above seem to reflect the reality of the Quelimane municipality in the aspects already studied, which allows us to affirm that PERPU did not contribute significantly to improving the living conditions of citizens in the Quelimane municipality over the period from 2014 to 2018, so that high levels of deprivation persisted, reflecting the high number of multidimensionally poor families in the municipality.

CHAPTER V: CONCLUSIONS AND RECOMMENDATIONS

5.1 Conclusions

To make PERPU a reality, the government has disbursed 10,350,790.00 meticais a year to finance small, medium and large income projects in the municipality of Quelimane. From 2014 to 2018, a total of 2,070 jobs were created, with a greater focus on trade in basic necessities.

PERPU was designed to complement the government's efforts to provide resources to citizens who are unable to go to the bank to take out a loan to finance entrepreneurial and income-generating initiatives for their survival.

What was found was that in the municipality of Quelimane, PERPU funds were not channeled to people and projects in accordance with the objectives of its design. It turned out that they were directed at individuals who already owned and run existing projects, i.e. many of these borrowers are looking for the fund to strengthen their businesses.

However, they would not be eligible for this fund, as it is understood that they have the minimum conditions to support their families. As stated in the conceptualization of poverty in the Plan of Action for the Reduction of Absolute Poverty (PARPA) (2001-2015), poverty is "the inability of individuals to ensure for themselves and their dependents a set of minimum basic conditions for their subsistence and well-being, according to the norms of society".

In the more specific case of decentralized and deconcentrated local authorities, these minimum conditions are assigned to local economic and social development, the environment, basic sanitation and quality of life, public water supply, health, education, culture, leisure and sport, local authority police, urbanization, construction and housing, in accordance with the Basic Law on Local Authorities, Article 6 of Law No. 2/97 (Law No. 19, 2007, of 28 May).

The social democratic conception on which this work is based will be reconciled with this perspective, since it is the state's responsibility to guarantee the welfare state.

The secretaries of the neighborhoods played a leading role in disseminating and instructing the granting of the funds made available by PERPU, with an emphasis on interpersonal communication.

It was also noted that the monitoring and evaluation process by PERPU managers has not been constant and cyclical. And that there are still no rigorous instruments guiding the repayment of the fund by borrowers if they fail to do so, which reinforces our perception of the poor performance of the local council in implementing PERPU in its territory.

However, it is clear that the situation of poverty in the communities does not seem to have been resolved, given the high levels of deprivation that certain urban families have been experiencing (not having access to quality basic public services and not being able to satisfy them by other means due to lack of financial capacity).

5.2 Suggestions

- The municipal council, in the process of selecting and approving projects, must take into account their sustainability and must accompany them in the implementation process.
- It should run awareness campaigns so that all residents and potential voters can compete on an equal footing in a transparent manner.
- Some of the objectives for which the program was created are losing their way. With regard to this finding, it is suggested that managers pay more attention to the objectives that guide the program.
- Create more viable, efficient and effective regulatory policy alternatives to guarantee the replenishment of the funds allocated to Borrowers.

Bibliographical references

Adolfo, M. P. (2016). *Public Development Policies: A Look at PERPU as a Women's Empowerment Strategy in the City of Lichinga. 2012/2014*. Lichinga: UCM - Faculty of Forestry and Wildlife Resources Management.

Agum, R., Riscado, P., & Menezes, M. (2015). *Public Policies, Concepts and Analysis under Review*. Brazil: Agenda Política Magazine.

Albuquerque, A. F. (2004). *Strategic Management of Internal Information in Small Businesses: A Comparative Case Study of Companies in the (Hotel) Sector in the Brotas Region - SP*. Sao Carlos.

Anonymous (n.d.). *Poverty: definitions and measures*. Rio de Janeiro: PUC - Rio.

Arnaca, F. (2015). *Urban Poverty Reduction Fund: Beira and Quelimane with worrying levels of reimbursement* . Onlinenoticias.

Azevedo, C., & Abdalla, M. M. (2013). *The Triangulation Strategy: Objectives, Possibilities, Limitations and Proximities to Pragmatism* . Brasilia: EnEPQ.

Bergue, S. T. (2013). *Strategic Management and Public Policies: Possible Conceptual Approaches and Necessary Distances*. Rio Grande do Sul: Double blind review.

Borges Jr, A. A., & Luce, F. B. (2000). *Emerging or Deliberate Strategies: a case study of the winners of the ADVB Top Marketing Award*. São Paulo: RAE - Revista de Administração de Empresas.

Bruchez, A., & Antônio, V. (2015). *Analysis of the Use of Qualitative Case Study and Triangulation in the Brazilian Business Review*. Brazil: UCS.

Carmo, H., & Ferreira, M. M. (2008). *Metodologia da Investigação, Guia para Auto - Aprendizagem*. Lisbon: Universidade Aberta.

Castilho, A. P., Borges, B. N., & Tanús, V. (2014). *ILES Itumbiara scientific methodology manual*. Itumbiara: ILES/ULBRA.

Corrêa, R. L. (1995). *Urban Space*. Brazil: Editora Ática.

Cortina, A., & Martinez, E. (2005). *Ethics*. São Paulo: Ed. Loyola.

Crespo, A. P., & Gurovitz, E. (2002). *Poverty as a Multidimensional Phenomenon.* Brazil: ©RAE- electronic.

Damião, A. P. (2014). Espaço *Urbano, Produção do Espaço e Segregação Socioespacial: o Espaço Urbano Capitalista e o caso de marília/sp.* São Paulo: Revista do Laboratório de Estudos da Violência da UNESP/Marília.

Del-Masso, M. C., Cotta, M. A., & Santos, M. A. (n.d). *Ethics in Scientific Research: concepts and purposes.* Brazil.

Estevão, R. B., & Ferreira, M. D. (2018). *Public Policy Analysis: a brief review of methodological aspects for policy formulation.* Brazil: HOLOS.

Feijó, J. (2017). *Research Methodologies in Social Sciences: Research Experiences in Mozambican Contexts.* Maputo: Escolar Editora.

Fernandes, J. A. (2011). *Importance of Strategic Management in Public Companies Case study Electra - Empresa Pública de Electricidade e água.* Lisbon: University Institute of Lisbon.

Freitas, M. C. (2010). *Poverty and Social Exclusion.* Coimbra: FEUC.

Freitas, W. R., & Jabbour, C. J. (2011). *Using Case Studies as a Qualitative Research Strategy: Good Practices and Suggestions.* Brazil: Lajeado.

Gil, A. C. (1999). *Methods and Techniques of Social Research.* Sao Paulo: Atlas.

Gil, A. C. (2008). *Methods and Techniques of Social Research.* Sao Paulo: Atlas.

Gonçalves, N. M., Rothfuss, R., & Morato, R. S. (2012). *The organization and occupation of urban space in the cities of the 21st century: impacts of Brazil's public policies of the 1990s on the right to come and go in the local environment.* Brazil: Amicus Curiae.

Gorczevski, C., & Mayer, G. S. (2015). *Some Considerations on Public Policies as an Instrument for Social Inclusion.* Brasil.

Guerra, E. L. (2014). *Handbook of Qualitative Research.* Belo Horizonte: COPYRIGHT.

Hasse Filho, J. (2006). *Gestao Estrategica: proposta de um modelo para a Agro Veterinária Timbó.* . Florianópolis : Federal University of Santa Catarina .

Huntington, S. (1994). *The Third Wave. Democratization at the End of the 20th Century.* São Paulo: Ática.

Lima, J. P., Antunes, M. T., Neto, O. R., & Peleias, I. R. (2012). *Case Studies and Their Application: Proposal of a Theoretical Framework for Research in the Field of Accounting.* São Paulo: Revista de Contabilidade e Organizações, vol. 6.

Lundin, I. B. (2016). *Social Sciences Research Methodology.* Maputo: Escolar Editora.

Maguenhe, C. Z. (2016). *Evaluation of the Implementation of the Strategic Program for Urban Poverty Reduction in the context of employment generation in the KaMubukwana Municipal District (2011 - 2014).* Maputo: UEM - Faculty of Arts and Social Sciences.

Maputo, M. d. (2011). *Strategic Program for the Reduction of Urban Poverty.* Maputo.

Marcondes, N. A., & Brisola, E. M. (2014). *Analysis by Triangulation of Methods: A Framework for Qualitative Research.* Sao Paulo: Univap.

Marconi, M. A., & Lakatos, E. M. (2003). *Introduction to the Methodology of Scientific Work.* Sao Paulo: A.S.A.

Martins, R. F. (1983). *About the Concept of Strategy.*

Nascimento, F. P. (2016). *Classification of Research. Nature, method or methodological approach, objectives and procedures.* Brasília: Thesaurus.

Neme, C. M., & Santos, M. A. (2012). *Ethics: concepts and foundations.* Bauru.

Nixon, F., & Walters, B. (2017). *Supplement to the State of World Population Report, Mozambique, 2017.* Maputo: UNFPA.

Oliveira, M. F. (2011). *Metodologia Científica: Um Manual para a Realizacao de Pesquisa em Administracao.* Catalao - Go: Federal University of Goias.

Piovesan, A. & Temporini, E. R. (1995). *Exploratory research: methodological procedure for the study of human factors in the field of public health.* São Paulo: School of Public Health - University of São Paulo - Brazil.

UNDP (2010). *Human Development Report: The Real Wealth of Nations: Pathways to Human Development.*

Rocha, J., & Zavale, G. (2015). *The Development of Municipalities in Mozambique. Cadernos e Estudos Africanos* . Cadernos e Estudos Africanos.

Santos, M. O. (S.d.). *Public Policies and Social Control: Decentralization after the 1988 Constitution.*

Sebrae (2008). *Public Policy: Concepts and Practices.* Belo Horizonte: Sebrae/MG.

Silva, B. A., Alves, B. d., & Oliveira, R. S. (2015). *Application of Strategic Management and Its Relationship with Organizational Culture in Small Business Administration.* Proceedings of the III ERECAD.

Silva, M. O. (n.d.). *Debate on poverty: theoretical and conceptual issues.* Brazil.

Souza, C. (2002). *Public Policy: Concepts, Typologies and Sub-Areas.* Luís Eduardo Magalhães Foundation.

Legal provisions

Law nº 19,/2007, of May 28 (Basic Law on Local Authorities).
Law no.º 19,/2007, of July 18 (Spatial Planning Law).
Resolution. nº 18,/2007, of May 30 (the "Territorial Planning Policy).

Milton Keynes UK
Ingram Content Group UK Ltd.
UKHW010851280324
440101UK00001B/178